The
Carl
Jung
Psychology
Test

The Carl Jung Psychology Test

EXPLORE YOUR INNER PSYCHOLOGY

Lily Yuan

This edition published in 2023 by Arcturus Publishing Limited
26/27 Bickels Yard, 151–153 Bermondsey Street,
London SE1 3HA

Copyright © Arcturus Holdings Limited

All rights reserved. No part of this publication may be reproduced, stored in a retrieval system, or transmitted, in any form or by any means, electronic, mechanical, photocopying, recording or otherwise, without prior written permission in accordance with the provisions of the Copyright Act 1956 (as amended). Any person or persons who do any unauthorised act in relation to this publication may be liable to criminal prosecution and civil claims for damages.

AD011084UK

Printed in China

 # Contents

Introduction to Personality Psychology p6

Chapter 1
How Do Personality Tests Work? p14

Chapter 2
Who Was Carl Jung? p24

Chapter 3
The Four Scales of the 16 Personality Types p34

Chapter 4
The Eight Cognitive Functions
(AKA Personality Drivers & Passengers) p44

Chapter 5
Jung's Psychological Types p70

Chapter 6
The 12 Jungian Archetypes
and Their Roles for Life's Stages p96

Chapter 7
Jung's Theories: How His Personality Types
Have Changed Throughout the Years p106

Conclusion p116
Personality Psychology Glossary p119
Further Reading into Jung's Personality Types p124
Index p126
Picture credits p128

Introduction to Personality Psychology

Introduction to Personality Psychology

Why do some people pair together so well, like peanut butter to jelly? Why do some conversations with people feel forced – almost like pulling teeth? Why do certain people work better as a team? How come certain personalities fare better as friends, and others have the potential for a romantic relationship? Who do we look up to, and why?

All in all, what makes you … you?

That's where personality psychology enters the scene. To study personality is to study the many, many factors that influence how you think and feel, through your unique biology and upbringing. How did your parents behave throughout your life? What was your environment like growing up? These are key questions personality psychologists ask.

> Note: This book uses the inclusive gender neutral 'they' when describing the 16 personality types and throughout the text.
>
> Carl Jung is referred to as 'he' throughout his biography and the text. Jung's personal quotes are all *in italic*.

How is it that some people become instant friends and others can never get on? Personality psychology holds the answer.

Some people knew what they wanted to be when they grew up as a young child. Other people go through numerous career path changes to finally figure out their calling, or decide to exit the working life altogether and opt to travel in a van. Why do our lives all look so different from one another? Because our personalities influence our decisions in so many ways.

The meeting of two personalities is like the contact of two chemical substances: if there is any reaction, both are transformed.

We're more alike than different because we're approximately 99.9 per cent identical in our genetic make-up. Did you know that we actually share around 98.7 per cent of our genetic make-up with chimpanzees, and 44.1 per cent with bananas (yes, the fruit)? And look how incredibly differently we behave! What does the remaining 0.1 per cent account for? You've guessed it – our *personality*!

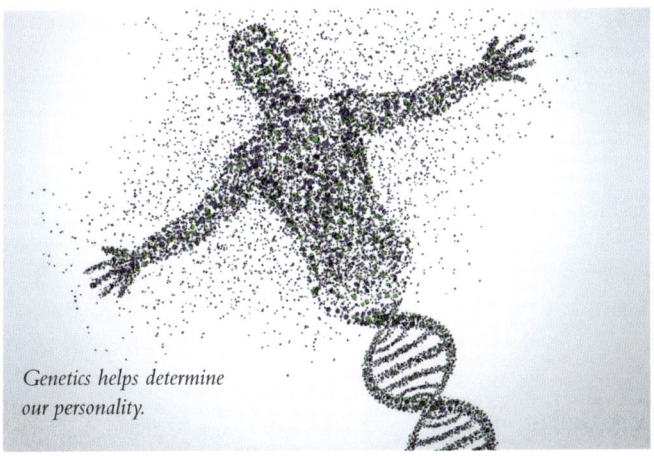

Genetics helps determine our personality.

Our personalities have a huge effect on our behaviour and the decisions we make.

In a nutshell, personality is the umbrella term for the traits, behaviours and preferences of an individual that stays *relatively consistent* over the course of time. It's closely linked with different branches of psychology: social, biological and developmental – to name a few. You may already be familiar with the terms *introvert* and *extravert*.

What happens when people face extraordinary amounts of stress? They can seem different from how they usually carry themselves. For example, someone who's more outspoken may seem uncharacteristically quiet after a stretch of challenging work, but after a while, they revert to their normal, bubbly self. Someone who's usually organized may seem scattered and clumsy in the same circumstances. Another person who usually makes decisions with facts and numbers may follow their heart when the situation calls for it. So, if you have a friend who's behaving differently than usual, it might be a good idea to check up on them and ask how they're doing.

One of the quickest ways to figure out your own personality is to take an assessment or test. Heads up – there's one included in your handy-dandy deck of cards! Skip to the end of this chapter for a quick breakdown of how to properly go about taking the Jungian personality test. It's easy to get the hang of it once you've gone through it a few times.

Stress can lead to us acting in uncharacteristic ways.

A short history of personality psychology

Way back in 1884, Sir Francis Galton proposed the fundamental lexical hypothesis, a linguistic theory that says that the personality traits most important and relevant to a group are eventually encoded into their language. The important characteristics are more likely to be neatly packaged as a single word, such as 'extraverted'.

In 1913, Carl Jung entered the conversation and began writing his first paper on personality types, which was published as *Psychological Types* in German in 1921 and then in English in 1923. In 1919, he introduced the term *archetype* to the world in his paper 'Instinct and the Unconscious'. We'll look more closely into his research on personality and archetypes further on in the book.

The notion of personality entered the mainstream around the 1930s with the issue of the quarterly *Character and Personality* in 1932. In 1936, psychologists Gordon Allport and Henry Odbert found almost 18,000 words in the dictionary that could describe someone's personality. From this list,

Francis Galton was one of the pioneers of personality psychology, coming up with a list of important personality traits.

they narrowed it down to 4,500 observable traits, which is still a huge number!

This brings us to one of the most popular personality trait theories today – the Big Five Factor Model (FFM), which has evolved over time. In 1946, Raymond Cattell used the model to generate 181 clusters of personality traits, which subsequently became the 16 Personality Factors model. In the 1960s, Air Force researchers Raymond Christal and Ernest Tupes found five recurring factors. Finally, P.T. Costa and R.R. McCrae went on to polish the FFM through the 1980s and 1990s.

The DISC is another popular personality assessment, and was developed by psychologist Dr. William Moulton Marston in the 1920s. It focuses on four main communication styles: Dominance, Influence, Steadiness, and Conscientiousness. The DISC assessment can help build stronger teams, and enhance personal and professional relationships. It is most often used in corporate settings, but can also be valuable in personal development, education, and therapy.

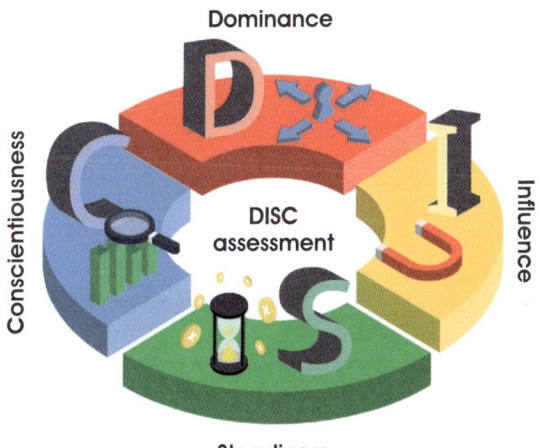

The DISC assessment is a popular model for personality testing.

How Do Personality Tests Work?

Now, how do personality *tests* work?

Personality tests are often scored on a *Likert scale* (i.e. a linear set of responses with increasing or decreasing intensity) of five choices – sometimes four if a 'neutral' option is omitted. They're similar to multiple choice answer quizzes you've seen in school – except there are no right or wrong answers! For example, they typically look like this:

Strongly Agree	Agree	Neutral	Disagree	Strongly Disagree
+2	+1	0	-1	-2

A Likert scale.

Certain questions correspond to certain psychometric outcomes, so the highest-scoring sections determine the strongest factors of your personality. You may have seen this format in surveys you've completed in school or at a grocery store! If you've been to see a psychologist, it's likely that you are already familiar with a questionnaire containing a Likert scale.

Psychologist Rensis Likert invented the Likert scale in 1932.

Personality trait theories, such as the Big Five (aka: Five Factor Model, OCEAN, NEO-PI), are based on factors *Openness* (O), *Conscientiousness* (C), *Extraversion* (E), *Agreeableness* (A) and *Neuroticism* (N). Trait theories use three criteria in testing: (1) consistency, (2) stability and (3) individual differences.

Here are some general descriptions of the Big Five factors:

Openness (O): Willingness to try new experiences (e.g. 'I'll try anything once!') and openness to different perspectives. People with high openness are often creative and risk-taking. They are definitely prone to having many, many hobbies and interests – a potential jack-of-all-trades!

Conscientiousness (C): Orderliness, responsibility and drive to complete tasks ahead of or on time. People with high conscientiousness respect rules, plans and schedules. They have their lives in order from head to toe. They're most likely the 'mum' or 'dad' of a group. Out of hand sanitizer at a restaurant? They've got extra handy.

Extraversion (E): Liveliness, energy and a general pull towards socialization and conversations with various people. People with high extraversion get a kick from making new connections and feel energized after being around people. When it comes to events and parties, they only have one requirement: the more, the merrier!

Agreeableness (A): The quality of pleasantness and co-operation. People with high agreeableness are kind, forgiving, trusting and altruistic. They're the loyal peacemakers of a friendship group – the ones people like and want to be friends with. Taken to an extreme, they can become a doormat.

Neuroticism (N): Tendency to worry or ruminate over events before, during and/or after they've happened. Strongly correlates to anxiety and depression. People with high neuroticism are hypervigilant and on edge. However, they've got street smarts and situational awareness. How's that for a survival buddy?

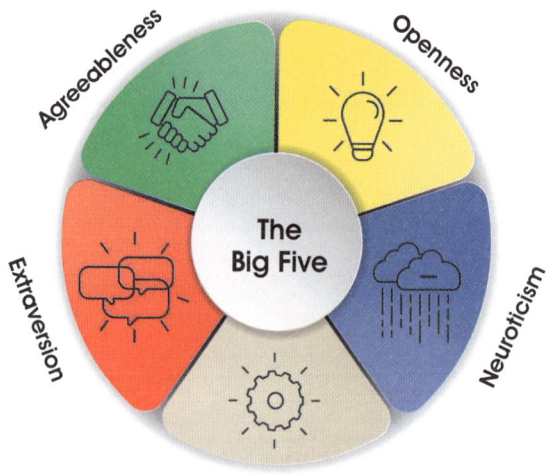

The Big Five personality traits.

This book, however, investigates Jung's *best-fit personality type theory* in greater depth, particularly his 16 personality types and eight *cognitive functions*.

A *Jungian function* is a pre-packaged mental process by which people think, feel, sense or intuit their actions. They come in a stack of four for each personality type – the strongest on top and the weakest at the bottom.

We'll take a closer look at Jung's functions in Chapter 4,

Personality traits can be incredibly varied. Personality type theories bring these together into coherent packages.

to explain the building blocks of his personality theory. We'll examine extraverts, introverts, sensors, intuitives, thinkers, feelers, judgers and perceivers in greater detail. If this all sounds like gibberish now, you'll get the hang of it later – pinky promise!

Personality type theories emphasize the different type categories into which people can fall. Personality types can be thought of as pre-packaged gifts that include a variety of traits and behaviours. For example, an introvert can come with general quietness, attention to detail, sensitivity to sound and excellent listening skills.

The categorization of different people according to their personality type is not a new concept. Back in 460–375 BCE, the Greek physician Hippocrates and his followers categorized people by the four humours,

The ancient Greek physician Hippocrates developed the theory of the four humours.

seasons and elements. Several centuries later, another Greek physician, Galen of Pergamon (129–216 CE), built on these theories and equated each of the four humours with a personality type, shown in italics below.

1. Blood/summer/air (*sanguine*)

2. Phlegm/spring/water (*phlegmatic*)

3. Yellow bile/autumn/fire (*choleric*)

4. Black bile/winter/earth (*melancholic*)

Sanguine loosely translates to cheerful and social; phlegmatic with calm and peaceful; choleric with aggressive and competitive; and melancholic with detached and pessimistic. Hippocrates believed people contained a 'blend' of all four humours, and that when they were heavily imbalanced, various illnesses and disabilities would ensue. Back then, people believed the colour of their vomit would determine which one of the four humours was overflowing. Now, we know that what we eat, and our overall diet can affect the colour of our bodily fluid, but so too can certain health

Until at least the Middle Ages, it was believed that the balance between the 'four humours' determined our personality and were responsible for our health.

conditions. For example, scientists have found that black bile only affects people who have chronic liver disease.

Continuing on with the topic of human bodies, William Herbert Sheldon (1898–1977) proposed a theory of three body builds in relation to personality type:

1. *Ectomorphs* (thin/reserved), who are introverted and highly sensitive.

2. *Mesomorphs* (muscular/assertive), who are powerful, competitive and aggressive.

3. *Endomorphs* (soft/easygoing), who are extraverted and relaxed with themselves.

You may already be thinking: 'Well, I know so and so and they're loud as heck, super competitive, and skinny! This other guy is ridiculously buff and goes to the gym every day – yet they're so

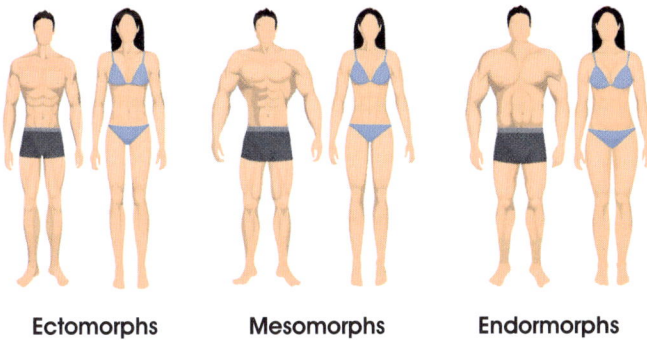

Ectomorphs   **Mesomorphs**   **Endomorphs**

The theory that body type – divided into ectomorphs, mesomorphs and endomorphs – determined personality once had many followers but has now been definitively debunked.

chill.' Rest assured: body build (also known as *somatotype*) theory has long since been debunked as pseudoscience.

Moving on – Carl Jung, the focus of this book, proposed eight cognitive types: (1) Extraverted Thinkers (ESTJ & ENTJ), (2) Extraverted Feelers (ESFJ & ENFJ), (3) Extraverted Sensors (ESTP & ESFP), (4) Extraverted Intuitives (ENFP & ENTP), (5) Introverted Thinkers (ISTP & INTP), (6) Introverted Feelers (ISFP & INFP), (7) Introverted Sensors (ISTJ & ISFJ) and (8) Introverted Intuitives (INFJ & INTJ).

We meet ourselves time and again in a thousand disguises on the path of life.

We'll get more into Jung's 16 personality types as you read through the book. They all have their unique strengths, weaknesses, ideal career paths and ways in which their intelligence shines. Have any questions about specific terms? Check out the glossary at the end.

We've only covered a few of the many personality type theories that exist here (just the tip of the iceberg!). There's still a whole fascinating world of psychological concepts for you to discover and learn. Welcome aboard the personality self-discovery train – hop on and prepare to discover the many colours of *you*! What better time to start learning about yourself than now?

For your information: included with this book you'll find a deck of 52 cards that contain the Jungian personality test, with a total of 28 questions.

To score the test, have ready a sheet of paper with numbers labelled in ascending order from 1 to 28. Work through the question cards in the correct order, answering by writing down A or B.

There are only 28 questions in total, and the entire test should take you around 5–10 minutes to complete. Feel free to take your time to read through and understand each question fully. Answer truthfully and try not to overthink your answers if you want to obtain the most accurate results. Remember, every personality type has its unique strengths and flaws.

The cards also provide useful, everyday advice for each of the 16 personality types, potential career matches, and frequently asked questions.

Share your results with a friend or colleagues, if you like. You can also read up on your personality type in greater detail in the latter half of the book, where there are many references to Jung's personality system.

As Carl Jung said,
'The world will ask who you are, and if you do not know, the world will tell you.'

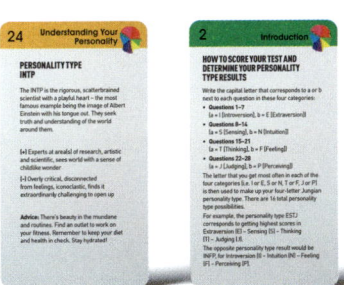

Who Was Carl Jung?

Chapter 2

Carl Gustav Jung (1875–1961), founding father of the 16 personality types and legendary Swiss psychologist, was born in Kesswil, Switzerland. He wrote the book *Psychological Types* in 1921. It has since skyrocketed in popularity in the workplace and been used in many counselling programmes.

Jung (pronounced 'young') sought to understand how different personality types interact with each other and, ultimately, how they affect society. He stated that no type was better or worse than another; all personalities have their respective strengths and weaknesses. We need people to be different, or else society is doomed to self-destruct and collapse!

> 'Your visions will become clear only when you can look into your own heart. Who looks outside, dreams; who looks inside, awakes.'

Carl Jung, a pioneer of personality psychology.

The small Swiss town of Kesswil, where Carl Jung grew up.

Considered one of the founding fathers of personality psychology, Jung was an eccentric psychoanalyst and psychiatrist who worked best alone. Indeed, he spent most of his childhood isolated (up until the age of nine) while he tinkered with his personal projects.

His dreams were psychologically complex and vivid – some of which frightened him as a child (and could now be classified as nightmares). These images that had defined his childhood slumbers became the foundation for his infamous archetypes later on. (We'll get more into that later in the book.)

When Jung was three years old, his beloved mother Emilie developed an unidentified mental illness that was severe enough for her to be temporarily admitted to a psychiatric ward. During this time, Jung made a greater connection with his father Paul, a Protestant Christian minister of the Swiss Reformed Church, and saw him as a role model.

Later, when he was 12, Jung was pushed to the ground by a schoolmate with such great force that he lost consciousness.

Ouch! After the traumatic incident, he would sometimes faint seemingly randomly while walking home from school or completing homework. Jung would later on learn that he had experienced *neurosis*.

Jung from an early age aspired to become a minister or priest, to follow in the footsteps of his father. Like father, like son? Not exactly. As he grew older, his spiritual approach and sole pursuit of God, without being shackled to notions of the state, religion or church, gave him the courage to tackle what 'truth' meant in his eyes. He had to figure it out for himself.

As he expanded his knowledge, he found many subjects to be fascinating, such as archaeology, paleontology, literature and philosophy. His wide range of interests made his educational specialization particularly challenging. It can be tough to be a jack-of-all-trades in a world that encourages you to focus on one thing professionally!

After a long period of pondering (★cue jazzy elevator music★), he finally settled on attending the University of Basel to study science and medicine, while simultaneously investigating mystical matters on the side. After successfully completing his degree, he joined the Burghölzli Clinic in Switzerland as an intern.

In 1905, Jung worked at the University of Zurich, where he remained as a faculty member until 1913. While there, he continued to

Jung studied science and medicine at the University of Basel.

Carl Jung at the Burghölzli Clinic, 1910.

build upon the complex and intricate personality theories he had expressed in his doctoral dissertation, 'On the Psychology and Pathology of So-Called Occult Phenomena', which he had written in 1902.

In 1906, Jung sent a copy of his book *Studies in Word Association* to Sigmund Freud (pronounced 'froy-ed'), the founder of psychoanalysis. That same year, Jung also sent Freud his book *The Psychology of Dementia Praecox*, an analysis of schizophrenia. It was too dense a read for a mainstream audience, but proved an intellectual treat to Freud, who then invited Jung to visit Vienna. The meeting took place in 1907.

Jung finally decided to remain psychologically independent from Freud as their theories (particularly Freud's role of sexuality in development) were too incompatible. Nevertheless, Jung proudly proclaimed, '*Freud was the first man of real importance I had encountered … no one else could compare with him.*'

In 1912, Jung published *Psychology of the Unconscious*, and ultimately steered away from Freud's more rules-heavy, deductive explanations, and sported a more mystical, intuitive approach. Jung believed the field of psychology to be highly complex and blurry instead of one plus one equals two. Sorry Freud: some friendships fizzle out naturally.

The two strikingly stubborn men reportedly had 'irreconcilable differences', which led to tension that eventually came to a head. Jung then proceeded to establish his concepts of archetypes, *complexes*, *synchronicities* and *the collective unconscious*. These highly visual concepts show up frequently in his dream analyses. Yes, he used psychic symbols to decode his patients' dreams as a psychotherapist!

Jung brought his theory of cognitive functions and types to light with the publication of his most famous work, *Psychological Types*, originally written and published in German in 1921. Newer personality assessments, such as Cattell's 16PF and the Minnesota Multiphasic Personality Inventory (MMPI), borrow ideas from Jung's psychoanalytic theories in their trait descriptions. He emphasized the alchemy of one's personality – how it could be transformed, energized or diminished.

Carl Jung had a fraught relationship with the other great psychoanalyst of the era, Sigmund Freud.

Jung's ultimate goal was to fulfill the wholeness of the human psyche and for each individual to truly '*understand thyself*'. To dig into what makes you, you. According to Jung, this is the one true key to growth and self-actualization. He suggested that many people were terrified of digging into the darker parts of their true selves and would rather live blind to their flaws than face them. How could someone reach their potential like that?

> *Until you make the unconscious conscious, it will direct your life – and you will call it fate.*

Carl Jung emphasized how personalities could change and transform, in a process he likened to alchemy.

Jung found inspiration from Eastern philosophies and religions like Taoism that helped him develop a unique approach.

His work was highly acclaimed by notable figures in both science and the humanities, such as psychologist Erich Fromm, psychiatrist Viktor Frankl and theoretical physicist Wolfgang Pauli. He eventually established his name in his field and joined the General Medical Society for Psychotherapy, and became president in 1933. Jung's influences from Eastern philosophy (Buddhism, Taoism, yoga) and Western faith (Christianity, Deism, Solipsism) bring forth a unique perspective that is studied by scholars, students and critics to this day.

The Four Scales of the 16 Personality Types

Jung's functions translate to four scales that make up 16 total personality types (which will be discussed in the next chapter). If you already know your four-letter best-fit type, feel free to skip to Chapter 5 and look for the subchapter containing your personality type. Otherwise, this chapter is a great place to start learning about the fundamentals of Jung's personality typing system.

PS: During the completion of *Psychological Types*, the final scale, Judging (J) – Perceiving (P), was a work in progress, with enough details to jump-start neo-Jungian personality tests such as the Myers-Briggs Type Indicator. The final scale deals specifically with how someone interacts with the outer world. You'll find more information on that in Chapter 7.

Jung broke down his personality typology into four attitude pair opposites. In other words, the personality trait opposites that we use in order to make sense of our reality. They go by the pair terms Introversion and Extraversion; Sensing and Intuition; Thinking and Feeling; Judging and Perceiving.

An example of a personality type is ESFJ, which stands for someone who prefers Extraversion (E), Sensing (S), Feeling (F) and Judging (J) in terms of Jung's attitude pair opposites. Their opposite type would be INTP, which stands for Introversion (I), Intuition (N), Thinking (T) and Perceiving (P).

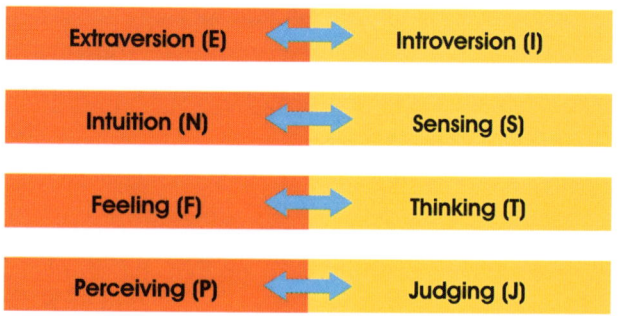

So, what do these terms all mean? Let's take a closer look.

To recap, there are four trait opposites or scales in Jung's 16 personality types:

Introversion (I) is the inclination to gain energy alone and be preoccupied with the internal world of thoughts, ideas and feelings. Decision-making happens alone.

People with strong Introversion are reserved, self-reflective, deep thinkers and great listeners. They prefer to be self-reliant with solo sports, solo travel and quiet activities such as reading. On a Friday night, they're likely cozied up at home, watching their favourite TV show or reading a book.

Extraversion (E) is the inclination to gain energy around other people and be preoccupied with the external world. Decision-making happens by getting others' opinions.

People with strong Extraversion are outspoken, approachable, excellent conversationalists and natural leaders. They prefer team sports, large parties and meeting new people. On a Friday night, they're likely out and about with their buddies, making new friends and searching for some action. The social butterflies, if you will.

Sensing (S) is the preference to take in information through the five senses: sight, touch, taste, hearing and smell; knowing through doing. To choose what's practical and reliable.

People with strong Sensing are down-to-earth, grounded, practical and realistic. They prefer activities that work with objects in the real world, such as sculpting, building and landscaping. Theories and abstract concepts confuse them and can even be deemed a waste of time or even useless.

Intuition (N) is the preference for hunches, 'a-ha!' moments and knowing through information and 'what could be' in terms of ideas. To foresee events and predict what'll happen.

People with strong Intuition are innovative, visionary, future-oriented and creative. They prefer activities that play with ideas, such as creative writing, meditation and improv. 'Common sense' and minute details can be difficult for them to grasp. They typically recoil at repetitive or monotonous work with little variety.

Thinking (T) is the preference to make decisions based on facts, pros and cons, and objectives. To remain emotionally neutral and logical.

People with strong Thinking are analytical, data-driven, logical and objective. They prefer using reason to solve problems and activities that make them think, such as playing board games, puzzles and coding. Conflicts and arguments are necessary for them to outline their opinions and express them in a rational manner.

Where wisdom reigns, there is no conflict between thinking and feeling.

Feeling (F) is the preference to make decisions based on how they'll affect other people, personal (subjective) values and how one 'feels' towards the situation.

People with strong Feeling are emotionally attuned, romantic

and idealistic. They prefer activities that channel their emotions, such as singing, dancing and spoken word poetry. Conflicts and harsh criticism can hurt them easily, and they spend a great deal of time trying to keep the peace within their social spheres.

Judging (J) is the preference to meet (sometimes beat) deadlines, schedule events in advance and view time as a finite (and important) resource. The follow through with what's been agreed on.

People with strong Judging are deliberate, organized, sometimes impatient and excellent planners. They prefer structured environments with clearly defined timelines and expectations to perform at their best. With arguments (which they view as necessary for progress), they prefer to have closure. A promise is a promise; their word is solid unless a true emergency comes up.

Perceiving (P) is the preference to keep options open 'in case' something better comes along, see deadlines as flexible and view time as an elastic resource. Everything is a 'maybe'.

People with strong Perceiving are more lax, easygoing, patient and adaptable. They prefer to 'go with the flow' and run with a project free from strict deadlines and defined to-do lists. They can stand messes, ambiguity and disorder, sometimes to the point when it becomes an issue. Think overflowing garbage bins and dirty laundry on the floors. Especially if a judger is in the picture as a roommate, oh boy!

Out with the Stereotypes!

The internet likes to exaggerate certain characteristics and make assumptions about certain personality types. For example, just because a person barely speaks during conversations and keeps to themselves, doesn't necessarily mean they're an introvert. Maybe they enjoy being a part of a group. The key thing to look for in extraverts is if they *gain* energy around people. On the flip side of the coin, a lively and loud person can still feel drained around people and hence be an introvert at heart.

 Everything that irritates us about others can lead us to an understanding of ourselves.

Here's another common stereotype: thinkers are rude while feelers are polite. While this may seem true on the surface, it's another misconception that gets thrown around a lot. A mature thinker can easily give off the impression that they're a feeler if they approach discussions in a civil manner. Thinkers who have to interact with many people may have perfected the art of emotional intelligence, which can give a 'feeling' impression.

In contrast, an immature feeler who has yet to learn how to control their anger outbursts and temper tantrums is anything but pleasant to deal with. Most children can seem like they prefer feeling at a young age, but their thinking takes longer to develop and show through their actions and during conversations. 'But I want it *NOW*! I'll scream and cry if I can't get what I need until you listen to me!' Stomp, stomp.

Let's not forget about the superiority complex surrounding intuitive personalities. Just because a person is an intuitive instead of a sensor, they're no 'smarter' or 'better' than them. There are

Children take longer to develop their thinking and have yet to learn how to control their emotions.

multiple ways intelligence can be seen through a person, such as being musical or naturalistic. We need people to be different and complement each other! Why else would there be so many different genres of music and subjects to learn?

There's way more to 'being smart' than just numbers (numerical) and words (linguistic). Yes, that's right: school was only part of the story. Jung said that every personality type has its strengths and weaknesses – we're all smart in our own ways. That's the beauty behind personality. If you look beyond the surface and really get to know someone, you'll discover how well-versed and intelligent they are in their subjects of interest.

Judgers and perceivers may appear to be the easiest to distinguish from Jung's attitude pair opposites. If they're organized, they're a judger. And if messy, they're a perceiver. Hold that thought. Judgers like to have things planned beforehand and work according to a schedule. Perceivers keep their options open and work in bursts. It's a person's work *style* that tells you their true preference.

There's more to the personality picture, though. On to Jung's cognitive functions … the missing puzzle pieces of our personalities.

Intelligence can take many different forms.

The Eight Cognitive Functions

(AKA Personality Drivers & Passengers)

The eight cognitive functions are the foundational 'building blocks' to Jung's personality typology. They're the pieces that make up our best-fit, four-letter type. Our first function leads our decisions, similar to that of a driver. It's the most mature, and one we're comfortable associating with ourselves. The one we may comfortably brush off as 'normal', and the one we get the most compliments for.

To begin, the *dominant* (primary) function is backed up by an *auxiliary* (secondary) function, and then the *tertiary* and *inferior* (fourth) functions. They can be extraverted (oriented towards the external world) or introverted (oriented towards the internal world). Picture the dominant function at the top of a function stack, with the inferior one on the bottom. Extraverts lead with an extraverted function, whereas introverts lead with an introverted function. The remaining function stack alternates between the two orientations. For example, an extravert has an extraverted – introverted – extraverted – introverted stack; the opposite

Jung's theory of cognitive functions can be thought of as a family car trip – the primary function is the driver, the secondary is the navigator and the other functions are the children sitting in the back.

holds true for introverts. Jung called the last (inferior) function '*infantile and tyrannical*'. In other words, like an angry toddler.

Think of it like a family car journey. The primary function acts as the driver of the Jungian psyche car, the auxiliary sits beside the primary (giving directions and suggestions), while the tertiary and inferior functions are the children who sit in the back seats and cry out in times of hunger, thirst and extreme bumps in the road. They can usually be distracted and consoled. Sometimes they may even have good ideas for the driver (who may fail to realize it at the time).

What about the *shadow functions* (the invisible ones below the four-stack)? Those troublemaking rascals are hidden in the boot or trunk of the car, and may only come out for a midnight snack or two. They're stashed away and rarely see the light of day, until some emergency crops up out of the blue. Out of fuel? Got a puncture? Out they come, then back they go to hide. Why are they even in the Jungian psyche car anyway? Because they're still a part of us, albeit a little shady.

 *Knowing your own darkness is the best method for dealing with the darknesses of other people.*

In terms of descending functional usage in our Jungian psyche car:

1. Primary (driver)

2. Auxiliary (passenger seat)

3. Tertiary (child – back seat)

4. Inferior (infant – other back seat)

The shadow functions are rarely seen, but they are still a part of everyone.

Jung states that functions that are neither dominant nor auxiliary (i.e. those shadow functions stuffed in the boot or trunk of the car) are expressed through the unconscious, such as in dreams. Repeating themes during a key point in life can indicate an important transition or breakthrough. Jung believed dreams can reveal information about the future, providing a crystal ball moment.

To confront a person with his shadow is to show him his own light. Once one has experienced a few times what it is like to stand judgingly between the opposites, one begins to understand what is meant by the self.

They are tied to various archetypes (or symbols) that represent stages of life, as well as repressed feelings and thoughts. (This will be discussed later in the book.)

The tertiary function is typically developed after mid-life, and the inferior function emerges under periods of deep stress. What about the functions below that? They crawl out of the psyche's shadows during psychological crises.

The unconscious is unfavourable or dangerous only because we are not at one with it and therefore in opposition to it.

To reiterate: extraverted functions (denoted with -e, such as Se) deal with the external world (our actions in the physical reality), whereas introverted functions (denoted with -i, such as Fi) deal with the internal world (the thoughts in our minds). Again, that's simply 'e' for external and 'i' for internal. Easy peasy.

Carl Jung believed that the shadow functions could reveal themselves in dreams.

From the Driver to the Baby in the Jungian Psyche Car

Jung proclaims, '*The primary function is the decisive factor.*' This function – the driver behind the wheel of one's personality (who happens to be the oldest and most mature) – ultimately decides where to go, when to stop and when to take a break. It does all the conscious manoeuvering, no GPS required. Its confidence is unmatched compared to the rest of the functions.

The auxiliary function, who sits in the passenger seat, holds the GPS and gives the driver instructions. It often makes suggestions that excite the driver, which is why they get along so well. It's so much more than just a passenger princess, however. It's got a huge degree of influence. However, keep in mind there are still two more passengers who sit in the back of everyone's Jungian psyche car…

Here comes a random bump in the road. The tertiary function, also known as the child, wakes up. It starts complaining. It's too hot in here. Can someone grab it a snack now? It's hungry. The music's too loud, the seat's in a weird position, etc. All of which immediately stresses out the driver. When our primary and tertiary functions get into an endless argument, it's known as a *stress loop*.

After an hour of the child arguing with the driver, the infant (inferior function) wakes up and starts screaming at the top of its lungs. The driver now can neither hear the GPS nor the requests of the child, and everyone gets cranky. That's the particular function that gets activated when we're in deep stress, also known as being in the *grip function*.

Jung's Comparisons Between Introverts and Extraverts

Jung also notes that introversion is shown through general *tension*, whereas extraversion is shown through general *relaxation*. The world can often seem too loud and busy for introverts, who need plenty of alone time to recharge. In contrast, extraverts can become bored and restless alone. Yes, they can be tempted to cause trouble as well if left alone for too long. That should be their warning label.

There is no such thing as a pure extravert or a pure introvert. Such a man would be in the lunatic asylum. Those are only terms to designate to a certain penchant, a certain tendency.

To visually highlight this distinction, Jung asks the reader to imagine an introvert in a peaceful, harmonious place. Think of a low-key park setting at dawn when most people are still asleep. Introverts can simply relax to almost resemble an extravert when they're with close friends and family. But remember – their temporary loudness and excitement is only reserved for a special few they trust.

However, when an extravert is stuck in a 'dark and silent chamber' (think e-learning for hours and hours alone during the pandemic), where their own thoughts can gnaw at them, they will be reduced to a state of tension and appear much like an introvert in their natural state: quiet, unassuming and focused while alone. These are extreme examples, according to Jung.

An introvert in a peaceful park, able to relax in the absence of noise and the distractions of other people.

An extrovert working at home, isolated, may be stressed by being left alone with their thoughts.

How can I be substantial if I do not cast a shadow? I must have a dark side also if I am to be whole.

The 16 types are split in half into eight categories or *cognitive functions*, each of which has a common name, for easier understanding:

1. Introverted Sensing (Si) – Recalling

2. Extraverted Sensing (Se) – Experiencing

3. Introverted Intuition (Ni) – Envisioning

4. Extraverted Intuition (Ne) – Brainstorming

5. Introverted Thinking (Ti) – Understanding

6. Extraverted Thinking (Te) – Evaluating

7. Introverted Feeling (Fi) – Internalizing

8. Extraverted Feeling (Fe) – Connecting

INTROVERTED SENSING (SI) – RECALLING

Bodily needs, aesthetic appreciation and symbolism in relation to the five senses are hallmarks of Si. The smell of a warm cup of mocha may bring back memories of reading in the library as an adolescent. The sound of a morning dove can turn time back to camping adventures as a child. The taste of an authentic dish can be reminiscent of an exotic vacation.

A familiar song playing in a supermarket may revitalize times spent driving alone in a car after spending time with a previous lover. Under stress, Si attempts to suppress and block out negative memories through the making of new ones in quick succession. However, the mind keeps count, and holds on to them whether it's emotionally healthy or not.

Si is an associative function, and places value and meaning on memories that may resurface unknowingly to the individual. Many musicians or poets have Si in their function stack, and are able to re-file their memories to produce emotionally accurate works of art; almost as if to 'relive' a moment in time.

Like a filing cabinet, data is passively stored away in the unconscious, to be used again when the occasion calls for it. It keeps an accurate and detailed list of important facts, dates and words locked in the depths of the mind, and sometimes spills out without warning (especially under stressful or dire situations).

How to develop your Introverted Sensing (Si): Go through old albums and yearbooks. Reflect on the moments from the past. Recall how things used to be and practise gratitude. Organize your belongings according to date or alphabetically. Collect knick-knacks that have memories associated with them.

Musicians are often introverted sensors.

Going through an old photo album can help you develop your introverted sensing.

The ISTJ and ISFJ personality types lead with Introverted Sensing (Si).

EXTRAVERTED SENSING (SE) – EXPERIENCING

Adrenaline junkies, thrill-seekers and athletes with high kinaesthetic intelligence use Se. The present moment, in all of its intensity, is of greatest importance, and reality is made through deliberate movement and thought. Manual dexterity and strength are important and emphasized by people who lead with Se.

Se takes in as much sensory information as possible from the environment to determine the next best course of action. If one option fails, a back-up will quickly be consulted and launched head-first into the real world. There's never a dull moment for Se, which is constantly on the lookout for action – good and bad. Ooh, look. A shiny object.

Se rapidly and automatically scans the immediate environment for possible opportunities or threats. It is proactive, quick to

Extraverted sensors are always searching for the next thrill.

react, and incredibly adept in emergencies. Its primary goal is to obtain instant gratification through the outside world. This may look like decadent foods, skydiving, stunt driving or bouldering.

Under stress, Se can look like indulging in unhealthy sensory pleasures such as alcoholism, escapism (e.g. binging reality TV, video games) and gluttony (overeating, especially foods that are considered delicacies). This tendency can be extraordinarily dangerous with personality types who have Se in the tertiary or inferior position of their function stack.

How to develop your Extraverted Sensing (Se): Move your body and break a sweat! Hone your reflexes and train

Engaging with the world through your senses – by smelling flowers, for example – can help you develop your extraverted sensing.

your strength. Take in the world with your five senses: smell the flowers, hear the many birds singing, taste the many flavours on your palate. Enjoy the moment; the present is a gift – soak it all in! You'll only be this young now.

The ESTP and ESFP personality types lead with Extraverted Sensing (Se).

INTROVERTED INTUITION (NI) – ENVISIONING

Elaborate visions for the future, 'a-ha!' moments and peak experiences are all pillars of Ni. It seeks wholeness, the greater picture, and ultimately the unity of the ever-perplexing nature of the world. It appears quite confusing to even close friends and family, and is the most misunderstood cognitive function.

Ni seeks to understand the entire state of affairs as a cohesive whole, to make predictions of what the future *will* (not *may*) be like. Similar to a biological cell, the nucleus is the core vision Ni has mapped out, and the supporting cellular organelles are the concepts that grow and interact to facilitate personal growth.

Flashes of creative brilliance and thorough understanding

The core of the introverted intuitive experience is the 'a-ha!' moment.

come to Ni, which appears strikingly different from any other function. Like an inspiration board, Ni collects what sparks its interest to propel an improved future with the infamous 'a-ha!' moment. It's supremely difficult to vocalize how said realizations have surfaced from the complex workings inside the mind.

Introverted Intuition is subjective in its functioning, and '*chas*[es] *after every opportunity in the teeming womb of the unconscious*'. To extraverts, it is lost in its own little world of fantasies, and easily loses track of time in the 'flow' state. Ni asks why one should live in the 'real world' when imaginary universes are far safer, more stimulating and utopian.

How to develop your Introverted Intuition (Ni): Keep a dream journal – what could your subconscious be telling you? Try envisioning the future, and what your life could look like. What do you see change? How and why will things be different? Write your thoughts down and come back to them after a set time to see what's changed.

Keeping a dream journal can develop your Introverted Intuition.

The INTJ and INFJ personality types lead with Introverted Intuition (Ni).

EXTRAVERTED INTUITION (NE) – BRAINSTORMING

Ne is all about new ideas, abstract connections and a stream of never-ending 'What if?' statements. It takes seemingly disparate subjects and ties them together with finesse. After all, what better way to understand the world than to play with ideas and concepts? There's always another point of view to research. The rabbit hole can always grow wider. Ne often shows up as youthful enthusiasm.

To the outsider, Ne appears wild, frenzied and slightly (read: extremely) nuts. In the midst of the mumbo jumbo of ideas, Ne wants to push the envelope of exploration and go *as far as it can* – there isn't even a box to begin with. Or maybe they've already broken the box and begun to create a new product out of it. Any crazy new theory is up for discussion; anything is on the table. Ne typically sees breadth over depth.

Brainstorming and making connections is an essential part of Extraverted Intuition.

Experimenting with art projects or trying out new hobbies can help you develop your Extraverted Intuition.

During conversations, Ne readily jumps from one tangentially related idea to the next without warning. Its energy seems 'jerky' or 'jumpy' compared to Jung's other functions. So, a chat about the latest superhero movie can bleed into the larger societal structures in play for the characters, which could then leap...

... straight to how a character's quirk reminds the person of another character in a different movie, which may then lead to a discussion of how movie directors differ from each other in the strangest ways. Which can then move the conversation to an interview with a certain director and what they said. Ne is random and rapid-fire, all the time. People with high Ne can whip up a list of ten completely unrelated concepts in under a minute. For fun.

How to develop your Extraverted Intuition (Ne): Try out new things – it could be a cuisine, hobby or even subject. Expand your tastes, let go of judgements, and embrace being spontaneous. Brainstorm fun activities with a friend. Experiment with different concepts: mixed media artistry, for example.

The ENTP and ENFP personality types lead with Extraverted Intuition (Ne).

INTROVERTED THINKING (TI) – UNDERSTANDING
As an iterative framework that seeks to boil elements down to their bare-boned fundamentals, Ti propagates and filters incoming information and sifts through inconsistencies with critical thinking. Ti is always open to debate, although *notoriously* difficult to convince or persuade. It requires mental clarity and definiteness over all else.

Inductive reasoning is preferred to deductive reasoning, as the missing links between abstract phenomena are unconsciously connected in the shape-shifting Ti web of ideas. New

Introverted Thinkers like to develop a complete framework of knowledge.

information must be analyzed *before* it can enter this malleable web. Ti constantly asks the question, 'How does this make sense to *me*?'

For instance, in the mastery of a subject, Ti wants more than just the facts – it needs to understand the underlying mechanisms, nuances and framework of the entire sphere of knowledge. This process, naturally, is long-winded and involves months (or years) of uninterrupted alone time to crystallize.

A series of experiments conducted in reality, after trial and error, helps Ti formulate larger patterns and laws to explain the unpredictable, chaotic and fluctuating nature of a reality destined towards entropy. The emerging fields of systems thinking and metacognition (thinking about thinking) are right up Ti's alley.

How to develop your Introverted Thinking (Ti): Learn how to think, and think how to think. Question what is, and why it is the way it is. Debate with a friend. Play strategy games. Keep questioning the reality of nature. Read books that deal with various cognitive biases or philosophies that can change your worldview.

Playing strategy games can develop your Introverted Thinking.

The ISTP and INTP personality types lead with Introverted Thinking (Ti).

EXTRAVERTED THINKING (TE) – EVALUATING

Proven methodologies, measurements and systems are Te's cup of tea. Te is a go-getter, and thrives under action and having things *work*. It seeks to optimize experiences, streamline procedures and categorize tasks to productively plough through each day. What better way to end the day than to have everything checked off the to-do list?

Schedules with specified end times and blocks help Te effectively streamline their day-to-day tasks. It prizes accolades, certifications and regimented academic programmes. Status symbols and recognitions also float the Te boat. Anyone with strong Te is likely to display an array of exceptional achievements collected through the years in their living space. Medals, trophies, ribbons … all that jazz.

Being recognized for achievements through prizes, certifications and promotions is a key motivator for Extraverted Thinkers.

Te is all about strategy and method, and thrives on continuous improvement to pre-existing systems. When faced with a problem, Te lays out a step-by-step plan in order to fix and mitigate errors as they occur in real time. In the end, it boils down to *if it works, it works*. The less time it takes to complete a project, the better. Just the facts, ma'am.

The cause-and-effect nature of the scientific method is a quintessential Te process, whereby any variables are clear, and an end result can be adequately measured. Te craves using applied knowledge (and seeing it work in reality) rather than refining what is already known. It typically fares well in traditional schooling methods.

How to develop your Extraverted Thinking (Te): Plan for (and seize) the day with a planner or calendar. Organize your workspace and workflow. Use facts and efficiency to

Use a day planner to develop your Extraverted Thinking.

make decisions. Most importantly, optimize your schedule. Put everything in its place and move through time with a sense of purpose. The pomodoro technique (a time management strategy that helps you alternate work periods of a set duration with scheduled breaks) is a great tool for productivity.

The ESTJ and ENTJ personality types lead with Extraverted Thinking (Te).

INTROVERTED FEELING (FI) – INTERNALIZING

Moral judgements, stone-hard values and clear likes or dislikes are what fuel Fi. It's fiercely protective of people and ideas it holds dear and perceives to be meaningful or important. On the

Introverted Feelers place inner peace above all else.

outside, it can appear cold, aloof and melancholy. Still waters run deep, and Fi feels emotions very deeply, but will hide them to avoid confrontations.

It seeks peace within itself first and foremost, and holds authenticity to the highest regard. In terms of behaviour, Fi appreciates consistency in values and ethicality above all. It can put itself in someone else's shoes when it's gone through a similar experience, therefore understanding the meaning of empathy.

Falling privy to 'nonsense' trends is akin to committing Fi suicide – as it would mean adopting the collective mindset or taste of popularity – a disappointment and betrayal to the true self. Fi sees being called 'weird' or 'different' as a compliment, instead of an insult, as Fe (see p. 68) would. It marches to the beat of its own drum.

Fi's values system may take years or decades to fully mature and solidify. After finally confirming said values internally, Fi then can make decisions and undergo actions that fully align with them with reassurance and certainty. Most notably, Fi must feel balanced within itself *first* to then be able to help other people. People with high Fi can take a long time to heal.

How to develop your Introverted Feeling (Fi): Share your personal feelings in the form of art – poetry, prose, painting. Write in a journal only you will see. How do you want to live more authentically to yourself? What are your most important values? Relate to others' stories by how you've experienced something similar to them.

The ISFP and INFP personality types lead with Introverted Feeling (Fi).

Sharing your feelings through art can help you develop your Introverted Feeling.

Extraverted Feelers like to fit in to groups and have no trouble reading the room.

EXTRAVERTED FEELING (FE) – CONNECTING

Community, intergroup harmony and the expansion of social activity characterizes the naturally outwardly giving nature of Fe. Naturally sympathetic and caring, Fe considers the well-being of the group over its own preferences. Sometimes this can evolve into overstepped boundaries and burnout from trying to please everyone.

Fe seeks to belong to a larger collective, a community of warm and supportive members. Common manners and social rules are also held highly by Fe. Chameleon-like in nature, Fe openly expresses sympathy for others' feelings. It can also *feel* what others are feeling at times, as Fe can 'read a room' with ease. We call this empathy.

Fe wants to fit in; to 'feel accepted' and not weird (or an outcast) by learning the unwritten rules of popularity. Others' actions, modes of communication, and fashion style may subconsciously influence Fe. It thrives on group harmony, acceptance and reassurance. What could possibly be worse than being labelled as an outcast or a reject?

At the core, Fe picks up subtle cues from the environment to know how to act in order to feel the reassurance they crave from external approval. Fe proudly wears its heart on its sleeve, and makes it known. However, Fe can also be a master actor, with its imitative superpowers … which can be used for the better or worse.

How to develop your Extraverted Feeling (Fe): Join a group to give back to the community. Learn the power of empathy and use this to connect better with others. Understand how to identify emotions and 'read a room'. Talk to more people and stand in their shoes! You can learn so much from the stories people have to share.

The ESFJ and ENFJ personality types lead with Extraverted Feeling (Fe).

Use your empathy and connect to others to develop your Extraverted Feeling.

Jung's
Psychological
Types

Jung's original work that sparked the 16 personality type revolution, *Psychological Types*, is a lengthy and complex read – the sixth volume of his complete work. His New Age focus on self-actualization (that is, the apex of understanding the true psychological self, popularized by American psychologist Abraham Maslow) helps shine a positive, optimistic light on human nature.

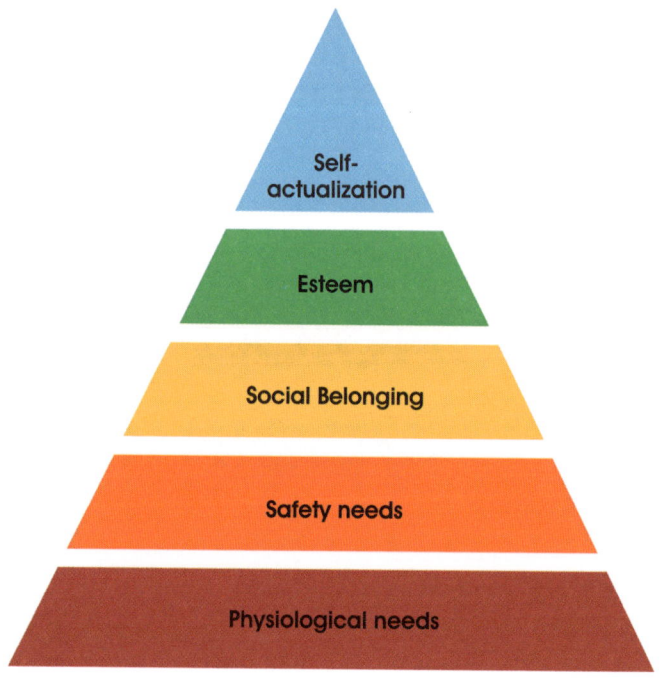

Abraham Maslow's hierarchy of needs, with self-actualization at the top.

Jung also tied in concepts from existentialism and humanistic theories to form the basis of his personality theories. To him, each person had one best-fit personality type to embrace

Carl Jung endeavoured to sort the multitudes that make up one's personality into manageable types that could be used as valuable tools for understanding ourselves.

and develop over time. Each personality type had strengths and weaknesses; everyone had something to bring to the table.

He worked tirelessly on his personality theories to help give others the psychological tools to understand themselves, rather than to directly teach them how to live or think, as do many philosophers. It's up to each of us to use our best self-judgement to figure out our best-fit personality type and use this knowledge for good.

To further help clarify his writing (which can be quite a challenging read, especially for individuals new to personality psychology), he included a detailed glossary at the end of *Psychological Types*. It contains more than 50 definitions, including some archaic or outdated terms. Many textbooks have updated the Jungian terms with modern lingo.

Jung saw self-typing as 'extraordinarily clouded'.

As a psychiatrist, Jung spent hours evaluating and communicating with his often confused – or even troubled – patients. He also emphasized the difficulty of self-typing, in which he claimed to be 'extraordinarily clouded' in the realm of knowing one's own personality. To know oneself is to go through a long journey of careful self-reflection.

Born and raised in a religious family, he even tied in principles from gnostic (that is, religious) philosophy with his eight psychological functions. This was one step forward towards his greater vision of understanding people's personality types. Jung saw the mysticism in our personalities and wanted to understand their many dimensions as deeply as he could.

*I am not what happened to me.
I am what I choose to become.*

In *Psychological Types*, Jung delivers an extensive, in-depth critique on personality type theory through history in relation to classical and medieval thought, poetry, psychiatry, philosophy and history. He touched upon the 'natural science' methods of German chemist and philosopher Wilhelm Ostwald, who coined the *classic* and *romantic* personality types.

He discusses the connections between his personality types and the four humours outlined by Galen that we covered in Chapter 1: *choleric* (yellow bile), *sanguine* (blood), *phlegmatic* (phlegm) and *melancholic* (black bile).

With respect to philosopher William James' opposite pairs, *rationalism* vs *empiricism*, Jung comments that this pair provides an incomplete view of *thinking*, which must be paired by his own conceptualized opposite, *feeling*. You can *think empirically*, as in the case with Intuitive Thinkers. You can also *feel rationally*, as Sensing Feelers do.

Wilhelm Ostwald divided personalities into 'classic' and 'romantic'.

Jung also disagreed with German philosopher Immanuel Kant's suggestion that 'the reason is the source of the idea', which is a purely introverted view. Jung suggests that extraverts' assumption of a schema (i.e. a general concept of an idea) is 'a mere arbitrary choice, or a generalization from limited experience', one that means they may be more prone to believing stereotypes.

All in all, Jung's view on psychic health is 'wholeness', a concept tied to understanding his thoughts on analytical psychology. In other words, there's an opposing aspect of light: darkness; we all have conscious and shadow functions. He reiterates the importance of Eastern and Western spirituality, and upholds a dynamic acceptance of the scientific and spiritual approaches to personality.

This proved to be too unorthodox and even controversial for other psychiatrists of his time, most notably for Sigmund Freud, as mentioned previously, who needed objective data and proof. This didn't stop Jung, though.

Jung emphasized the idea of 'wholeness' when it came to understanding mental health.

The Extraverts

EXTRAVERTED THINKERS
ESTJ & ENTJ – led by Extraverted Thinking (Te)

Extraverted Thinkers are actively looking for solutions and problems to solve. They prefer to think in terms of productivity and maximizing their goals, while discussing in teams. When they're looking for a solution, it must always be backed up with objective data. If religious, Extraverted Thinkers will be the influencers of a faith and encourage other members of the congregation to follow the rules accordingly.

This rigidity and seriousness can scare or intimidate other personality types if they're unhealthy. Extraverted Thinkers gravitate towards positions of power or influence where they can socialize with many people. They relish an audience who values their opinions and time and can contribute to important occasions. The world needs leaders of all kinds, and Extraverted Thinkers make great candidates.

The ESTJ learns by executing their well-defined plans. They value productivity and hard work and will not back down when they have to remind someone to improve their work ethic. The ESTJ sticks to their word and carefully planned schedules and will respect others who value their time. While strict and sometimes bossy to strangers, they have a secret soft side for their loved ones.

The ENTJ thrives on execution and aims to put their work out in the world – through blogs, podcasts and seminars. They prioritize their day-to-day tasks and enjoy learning how to better manage their time, finances and resources. The ENTJ always comes prepared with meeting notes and an agenda to discuss with their team. They feel best after a long day (or night) of hard

Jung's Psychological Types 79

Extraverted Thinkers like to put their ideas out into the world, but need to be mindful of potential burnout.

work and seeing their efforts unfold smoothly and efficiently.

Practical advice for Extraverted Thinkers: Slow down and learn the value of rest and relaxation. You'll burn out if you put your work over your health, sometimes in a flash. Let go of what you cannot control at the end of each day. Meditate if this helps you clear your mind when you wake up. Again, give yourself permission to rest! Sleep on it if you have to and work on something the next day if you're already exhausted.

EXTRAVERTED FEELERS
ESFJ & ENFJ – led by Extraverted Feeling (Fe)

To err is human; to forgive, divine. Extraverted Feelers typically have several mantras they repeat daily, and strive to be a better person, to ultimately help society in some way. They want to care for and understand other people; to share their teachings and empathize deeply. However, their thinking can easily be clouded by their feelings and how their actions may impact others.

Extraverted Feelers think as they feel and seek rapport from their environment. So, the harmony and happiness of the group is of utmost importance. They can easily 'feel' how characters in a movie do, and may burst into tears, fully immersed in the moment. Introverted Feelers, in contrast, would have to personally relate to a character to be moved to the same degree.

The ESFJ keeps a mental checklist of special events coming up: anniversaries, birthdays, holidays … the list (and life) goes on and on. They probably have a planner or magnetic calendar of sorts to keep all of their friends' and family members' important dates. To the ESFJ, staying connected and giving to their community is what truly matters. They enjoy being on top of trends and finding out what's cool or hip in their social spheres.

The ENFJ has their mind set on their wider community and hence improving the lives of others. Altruistic and philanthropic

Extraverted Feelers like to give back to the world through community engagement and helping society and others in whatever way possible, but they should also remember to help themselves too.

Extraverted Sensors look for stimulation wherever they can find it, but should remember to keep an eye on their health, too.

at heart, they make great teachers and non-profit managers with a strong, empathetic drive for a better tomorrow. The ENFJ can buckle under conflict, which causes an enormous amount of stress for them. With self-care and time, they can learn to be a peaceful yet impactful force for good, all while implementing healthy boundaries.

Practical advice for Extraverted Feelers: Treat yourself like a best friend and practise self-care. Avoid emotional burnout by setting boundaries and saying 'no' if necessary. Be kind but firm when you request time to heal and rejuvenate. Take time to practise immersing yourself in solitude and finding peace within yourself. It's not 'selfish', as you may have believed. It's crucial for your mental health.

EXTRAVERTED SENSORS
ESFP & ESTP – led by Extraverted Sensing (Se)
You only live once. And Extraverted Sensors fully soak in each moment with all of their senses, making them excellent athletes, emergency responders and stunt actors. As true connoisseurs of life, what you see is what you get. Extraverted Sensors accumulate experiences and move towards excitement. Sometimes this may result in reckless behaviour or addictions to chase a new high.

The present is what truly matters to them – they'll readily take the moment and make it their version of perfect. This could mean reaching out to a new person in order to gather information for an idea. Or perhaps a stimulant for that extra energy boost in order to plough through a project. Whatever it is, Extraverted Sensors constantly have all gears going in their minds – it's full speed ahead.

The ESFP is the life and soul of the party. They always have a never-ending series of stories to share with others and want to relish every bit of life. They're happy to try anything once and have outstanding conversational skills that can hook just about anyone. They may, however, experience burnout with their lavish lifestyles: health-wise or financially. When the ESFP is in a good place, they truly appreciate each moment as it is and encourage others to do so as well.

The ESTP is a kinaesthetic learner to the core and thrives on action. There's never a dull moment for them – they go wherever the excitement calls. Cool and logical, their moods typically remain stable through the day. The ESTP can adapt to the pace of each moment, which is a highly valuable skill for activities that require dexterity and agility. It's common for them to take time off from work for sports-related injuries, but once they're back – they're back!

Practical advice for Extraverted Sensors: Your body keeps score of the artery-blocking fast food you consume and all-nighters you pull! Keep your health in check; your mind and body will thank you in the long run. Consistency is key for you – even 20 minutes for a quick meditation and light jog will add up. Encourage your more introverted friends to chase their dreams and take chances. They'll appreciate your support a thousand times over.

EXTRAVERTED INTUITIVES
ENFP & ENTP – led by Extraverted Intuition (Ne)

Like a kid in a candy store, Extraverted Intuitives want to try out anything and everything interesting (whether smart or silly). They relish conversations with other people and bouncing around their ideas. They're always on the lookout for new, promising opportunities and can quickly run with (and abandon) an idea. They can see their life heading in many directions at once and are prone to changing their career paths frequently.

In relationships and friendships, they see 'what could be', and

Extraverted Intuitives thrive on good conversations, but sometimes need to remember to get a second opinion before getting too caught up.

may lose sight of who a person truly is – causing insurmountable issues down the road. Extraverted Intuitives can easily see the potential in a person and how much they could improve in the future. However, people are multifaceted and anything but a DIY project. This kind of thinking works better with practical solutions and a sensible team to pull them back to earth.

The ENFP thrives in environments where they can be their authentic self, while being able to explore exciting possibilities. They enjoy connecting with others and working on multiple projects at once to keep their minds fulfilled and inspired. As a creator at heart, the ENFP relishes in chances to tread through the human condition with freedom. Their childlike naivety and wanderlust may lead to procrastination at times, however.

The ENTP is a devil's advocate, the debater and joker of the 16 personalities. They have equal parts wit and charisma, and can easily brainstorm ten topics to discuss from off the top of their head. Above all, they crave influence and a lucrative possibility, which, when immature, can lead them to risky gambling habits. The ENTP is a natural candidate for entrepreneurship and the world of venture capital, with their hard and soft skills.

Practical advice for Extraverted Intuitives: Get a second perspective (or two!) to help ground and evaluate your ideas. Your many notions need to be organized and executed properly. Stick to a healthy routine to generate better ideas and reduce stress. People seek leaders within the workplace and in friendship circles to ramp up the positive energy and ideas. Heads up – it's your chance to shine!

The Introverts

INTRODUCED THINKERS
ISTP & INTP – led by Introverted Thinking (Ti)

Trial by error. Introverted Thinkers are natural troubleshooters, either through practical matters or when theorizing. As natural sceptics, they want to fully understand how the world works – how each part relates to the whole – and seek the truth. Introverted Thinkers spend most of the time in their heads to work through life's toughest questions and paradoxes. It can be challenging to relax when their brains are thinking and reasoning all the time!

Sometimes this means hours of scouring through academic papers and textbooks to dust off emotional judgements and fluff. Through their quest for truth, they strive to polish their diamond of knowledge to perfection. Many famous poker players are thought to be Introverted Thinkers, with their dynamic strategies, from placing bets to calling bluffs. Introverted Thinkers thrive as researchers and philosophers, as they need autonomy and focused time alone.

The ISTP wants to experience events first-hand with all five senses. They learn from diving into a situation without guidance, making mistakes (and fixing them) as they go. The ISTP learns and picks up skills quickly, which makes them exceptionally suited to the skilled trades, such as woodworking or carpentry. They may appear aloof to strangers and hard to get to know, which can hinder their potential opportunities for friendships or relationships.

The INTP is the rigorous, scatterbrained scientist with a playful heart – the most famous example being the image of Albert Einstein with his tongue out. They can easily lose track

Introverted Thinkers love to think through tough problems and engage in deep research, but sometimes need to be reminded that research should be applied to the real world, too.

of time and neglect basic necessities such as nourishment when waist-deep in their research. The INTP relishes in ideas, however strange and far-fetched they may appear. Sometimes INTPs may fall into a rabbit hole of procrastination by fleshing out an idea in their head, rather than in reality.

Practical advice for Introverted Thinkers: Put your ideas to work in the real world. Yes, that means you have to *apply* them instead of purely researching for the sake of it. How? Find a small but mighty team of people who share your vision. You may find clarity when you take walks, hit the gym or participate in a solitary sport. Give yourself permission to *feel* emotions, however illogical or unnecessary they may seem at the time.

INTROVERTED FEELERS
ISFP & INFP – led by Introverted Feeling (Fi)

'That's just the way I am', sings Charlie Puth. Introverted Feelers thrive on authenticity and being true to themselves. They often hold strong feelings with a stoic expression to the outside world, like lightning in a bottle. However, when they truly feel an emotion and are comfortable with their surroundings, they'll show it to the world with a toothy grin. They're constantly categorizing people, experiences and things into 'likes' and 'dislikes' accordingly.

The dream? To put their feelings into art and keep creating for as long as they live. Introverted Feelers abide by their core morals and make them known, usually quietly through their lifestyle choices or loudly in a bout of rage if they feel threatened. Many artists vocalize their feelings through song lyrics, roles they play on stage or even through images hidden in brushstrokes. Many (not *all*) historical starving artists are thought to have been Introverted Feelers.

The ISFP proudly makes their individuality known through

Introverted Feelers often make great artists, but sometimes need a little encouragement to step outside of their comfort zone.

their fashion and lifestyle choices. They're highly in tune with their feelings and can easily relate to others' stories with how they've experienced a similar situation themselves. Instead of following trends, they're happy to march to the beat of their own drum and own their quirkiness. The ISFP, in the midst of finding themselves, may be prone to excessive spending habits for what they enjoy at the moment.

The INFP may be the most reluctant of all to engage with personality type theory and refuse to be 'labelled' or 'stuffed in a box' with other people. Their individuality is less outwardly flashy and more inwardly focused, with daydreams and visions running through their minds constantly, although they appear outwardly calm. The INFP generally gets along well with others but may run into trouble when they encounter emotional distress or rigid authority figures.

Practical advice for Introverted Feelers: Be brave and take the chance to connect with like-minded individuals. Step outside of your comfort zone, one baby step at a time. Chunk your time efficiently and use a timer as you need it. Apply for the internship you've always dreamed of, because the first step to making your dreams come true is to literally make that first step. Befriend uplifting, protective and positive people who'll encourage you to shine.

INTROVERTED SENSORS
ISFJ & ISTJ – led by Introverted Sensing (Si)
Relaxed and organized, Introverted Sensors are the dependable, responsible worker bees of the 16 personalities. They thrive on predictability and routine, and become an integral part of their social circle(s). Their schedules and actions are typically predictable – sometimes to a tee. Traditional schooling and work structures are made for them, as the ISTJ and ISFJ are reportedly

the most common personality types.

Introverted Sensors have a keen eye for tradition and mannerisms that allow them to integrate into society swimmingly. Their trustworthiness and reliable nature make them easy to get along with. They work well with most people and understand the need for the mundane in order for life to function. In the workplace, they're likely to stick with a company for many years. When they order food, they have a few staple dishes and places they enjoy revisiting.

The ISFJ upholds tradition and likes to serve others, which gives their lives a sense of purpose. They keep their loved ones dear to their hearts and value family and loyalty over everything. Although the ISFJ is usually soft-spoken and agreeable, they will bravely stand up to people who bully the ones they love without hesitation, as they value treating others the way they'd like to be treated. You can always count on an ISFJ to keep a secret.

The ISTJ takes on each day with a serious, organized attitude. Their strong work ethic is unmatched in the office, and they often take home the 'employee of the month (or year, or decade)' award. They can store massive amounts of details and information in their brains and excel in careers such as law, accounting and medicine. One prominent issue? The ISTJ will chafe at change and sees it as unnecessary (if it ain't broke, don't fix it).

Practical advice for Introverted Sensors: Let your inner child come out to play at times – make some room for play and relaxation. Your quiet strength and loyalty is noticed by others, and you should be proud of yourself. Hang out with friends who encourage you to try new activities and expand your worldview. You deserve to feel happy and excited about life after all the work you've put in, busy bee!

Introverted Sensors can thrive in responsible professions like medicine and the law, but sometimes need reminding that there can be room for playfulness, too.

Introverted Intuitives can have flashes of brilliance, but sometimes need to remember that the mundane things in life are necessary, too.

INTRODUCTION INTUITIVES
INFJ & INTJ – led by Introverted Intuition (Ni)

Jung was considered by many scholars and psychologists to be an Introverted Intuitive (although he himself claimed to be an Introverted Thinker). While the inner minds of Introverted Intuitives are rich and bustling with inferences and flashes of brilliance, they can appear 'out of it' and neglect practical matters.

Introverted Intuitives may be perplexing even to their closest friends and family. They align themselves to their mission or greater vision, and can be prone to subjectivity. Their minds work constantly, piecing together information, mostly subconsciously. When they finally arrive at a conclusion, it can abruptly appear out of nowhere like a psychic realization or an 'a-ha!' moment.

The INFJ, a kind soul and master empathizer naturally interested in human behaviour, is less in tune with their own emotions as they can mentally absorb the atmosphere or 'vibes' of a room. Their quest for harmony can result in overstepped boundaries, anxiousness and perfectionism in their idealized relationships. However, when emotionally mature, the INFJ's high sensitivity, emotional intelligence and kind heart will help them discover and maintain deep, genuine connections.

The INTJ is all about strategy and mastery of a subject. With perseverance and a strong vision, they can bulldoze through every (real and imagined) obstacle to reach their goals. Although often brilliant and charming, their insights may come across as long-winded or confusing for others as they attempt to explain their research to a wider audience. Like the INFJ, they too battle with perfectionism, except more so in their knowledge and intellectual competence.

Practical advice for Introverted Intuitives: Your mind is *always* running on all cylinders. Sometimes you'll forget to shower or do your laundry … again. Let go of your need for perfectionism: done well is better than never done at all. Choose healthier foods, plan to exercise, and get some fresh air every day.

The 12 Jungian Archetypes and Their Roles for Life's Stages

What do you call a visual image of a symbol that embodies traits that relate to the human core? To Jung, these were his *archetypes*. These are different from his cognitive functions (the drivers and passengers we've discussed before) in that people contain a blend of all archetypes. The core four Jungian functions in our stack are fixed according to our best-fit personality type. By contrast, the strength of each archetype changes by age and important events through life, such as moving out of home or marriage.

For Jung, the elusive concept of the *persona* was that it is the social mask people wear in public to conceal certain parts of the true self, completely different from one's true personality. It typically aligns with the *ego*, sometimes *superego*, and shields the darker depths of the *id*. These terms relate to Freud's three-part psychoanalytic personality (id, ego and superego).

Carl Jung saw the persona as the social mask that people put on to face the public.

The first and most primitive and instinctual part of the psyche is known as the id. It operates on the pleasure principle and seeks to fulfill basic needs and desires without regard for morality or social norms. The ego, which is the second section, functions as the rational and conscious part of the psyche that mediates between the demands of the id and the constraints of the external world.

The last component – the superego – is the moral and ethical component of the psyche that internalizes the moral standards and values of society. It operates on the morality principle and seeks to uphold social and cultural norms, often through feelings of guilt or shame. Together, the three interconnected structures make up the human psyche according to Freud.

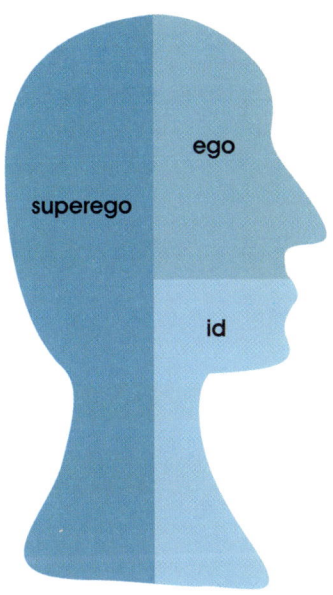

Freud divided personality into three components: the id, ego and superego.

The first half of life is devoted to forming a healthy ego, the second half is going inward and letting go of it.

Many id outbursts can appear impolite, childish and even controversial to an observer, so the persona works to effectively hide these from the world. A person may even become so bound to the persona that the true self is lost. Many actors experience this when they become too intertwined with a role they play.

Jung stated that his archetypes exist in a '*psychic system of a collective, universal and impersonal nature*'. They mark the different drivers behind human *motivation*. In other words, the archetypes are the little angels or devils sitting on our shoulders, telling us what we should do to be satisfied. Listen to these thoughts with caution.

He proposed that '*a group experience takes place on a lower level of consciousness than the experience of an individual*', as mob psychology would suggest. When we 'go with the flow', or simply follow what's popular, it takes less conscious thought to make decisions.

We are naturally drawn to certain archetypes, and repelled by others. Their symbolic meanings helped Jung analyze his patients' dreams and counsel them. He believed that key archetypes would appear at decisive ages in everyone's lives. For instance, the transition to adulthood from adolescence is a critical marker in a life path.

The four cardinal orientations

There are four cardinal orientations in Jung's archetypes:

1. Ego – To make one's presence known and admired.

2. Order – To maintain structure in societal settings.

3. Social – To foster genuine connections with others.

4. Freedom – To break free from physical and psychological limits.

THE 12 JUNGIAN ARCHETYPES

A person who repeatedly sees an explorer in their dream as a teenager may be called to chase a more off-road career path. Perhaps a travel photographer or blogger is in the stars for their future. A different individual who dreams about a caregiver may want to pursue a job that allows them to help others, such as a nurse or mental health counsellor.

The 12 Jungian archetypes are as follows:

1. Caregiver (Order)
   Seeks to help others, give freely and be recognized for their undying care and dedication – others' happiness is theirs as well.

2. Creator (Order)
   Expresses their authentic thoughts and feelings through a multitude of projects – work is their lifeblood.

3. Ruler (Order)
   Imposes order and control upon their world by upholding an orderly life to retain power.

4. Explorer (Freedom)
   Escapes to focus upon the next adventure and be proud to discover new findings all on their own.

5. Innocent (Freedom)
   Retains their wide-eyed, childlike wonder and naivety to block out threats and live in their imagined utopia.

6. Sage (Freedom)
   Seeks the truth and wisdom to understand all of life's mysteries in order to find their way to lasting peace.

7. Hero (Ego)
   Fights for justice and the greater good, all while testing their true character through hurdles and roadblocks.

8. Magician (Ego)
   Fills their mind with psychological tactics to influence people from their core and transform situations.

9. Outlaw (Ego)
   Destroys and reinvents the wheel for laws they personally see as being unfit or unreasonable to challenge norms.

10. Jester (Social)
    Enjoys all life has to offer without mental or physical bounds, and savours the present above all; the past and future are mere illusions.

11. Lover (Social)
    Ignites and feeds the flames of lust to chase an emotional high (over and over again) to experience bliss.

12. Member (Social)
    Values tradition, loyalty and safety to fit into society seamlessly and honours community rules and regulations.

All the most powerful ideas in history go back to archetypes.

Each individual, according to Jung, is said to have a complex blend of a few of the 12 Jungian archetypes, which can gradually develop and change over time due to their life circumstances and personal growth. Once a jester (childhood class clown), always a

The 12 Jungian Archetypes and Their Roles for Life's Stages 103

The 12 Jungian archetypes.

jester? Maybe, maybe not. It depends. Perhaps they went on to pursue freedom (explorer), or seek romance (lover)?

These archetypes provide general explanations for our various methods of feeling and reasoning. They are part of a *collective unconscious* – a pool of psychic images that are known to everyone. In storytelling and character creation, these archetypes can definitely come in handy. You probably can already think of a boy who falls under the Magician archetype (hint, hint: snowy owl).

Brand personalities in advertising psychology often use Jung's archetypes to paint an image of what a product or service should entail. Furthermore, consumers and users are also loosely grouped into personas. There's a level of mysticism in the evolution of technology as well – human-like chatbots, anyone?

For example, Coca-Cola's short new slogan, 'Real Magic', embodies the Magician archetype. The slogan implies that the next moment can be better, more *magical*, after drinking Coke. Advertising agencies are experts at the art of pairing words with a feeling, using many of Jung's concepts.

All consumers hold purchasing power, and what people buy and own can become a part of their identity. Possessions may not define a person, but they can certainly give clues to their personality. Jung's archetypes are influential in the way they dig down to core human *motivations*, which are the root of action.

A brand can methodologically list all the wonderful perks of their product, but if the consumer cannot be persuaded or 'hooked' on to it, then the purchase fails to close. The sale never happens. Why? The *feeling* has to be there for the marketing magic to happen. For Coke, it's the alleged magic.

Jung claimed that personas are conceptualized from a biological rather than a cultural background. They are instinctual and unswayed by the environment or one's upbringing. Again, this is all part of the collective unconscious; a database of symbols that explain why we're drawn to certain things and repulsed by others.

Latter-day research shows the massive role that peer influence and social media play in people's decision-making processes. Sometimes culture is strong enough to persuade people to betray or sacrifice core motivations in favour of outward approval. Since all the archetypes are hidden in our collective unconscious, could unconscious factors be influencing how they show up and change our behaviour?

Advertisers often divide their audience into groups based on Jung's archetypes.

Jung's Theories:

How His Personality Types Have Changed Throughout the Years

Jung wasn't the only researcher to propose personality theories. Some contemporary and many subsequent psychologists and thinkers also had ideas, many of which were influenced by Jung's work. He may be a staple figure in every psychology course and textbook, but there are many more 'neo-Jungians' to talk about!

 # The Myers-Briggs Type Indicator[1]

Mother-daughter duo Katharine Cook Briggs (1875–1968) and Isabel Briggs Myers (1897–1980) were the two women masterminds behind the famous Myers-Briggs Type Indicator, or MBTI® for short. The main difference between their thinking and that of Jung was that the pair believed personality reflected inherent abilities (fixed mindset), while Jung only saw preferences.

Cook's personality research garnered great support from her daughter Isabel when World War I began. The bright-eyed Briggs Myers (who self-identified as INFP) had ample time to dedicate towards perfecting the career-sorting assessment as she was not serving in the military and did not have other employment responsibilities at the time. She saw a gleaming, once-in-a-lifetime opportunity to help thousands – even millions – of people with their career paths.

Katharine found tremendous insight in Jung's *Psychological Types* (the 1923 English translation), so she contacted him personally, and even convinced him to meet up with her to chat in

1 Myers-Briggs® and MBTI® are registered trademarks of the MBTI Trust, Inc., which has no affiliation with this book.

Katharine Cook Briggs and Isabel Briggs Myers.

the United States several years later, in 1937. Before that meeting took place, she wrote a long-winded and descriptive child-rearing essay, *Meet Yourself Using the Personality Paint Box,* in 1926.

In 1943, the first version of the MBTI® was created and tested on students at Swarthmore College, where Isabel Briggs Myers was a volunteer counsellor. The pair's original personality sorting test had a total of 172 questions and 16 potential results (i.e. the 16 personality types). Myers and Briggs' goal was to help people thoroughly understand their personalities in order to make a positive change in the world. They saw a bright future in the workplace with more productive and happier employees.

During this decade prior to entering the market, Katharine and Isabel engaged in a practice known as 'type watching', which involved observing people's behaviour and attempting to categorize them according to Carl Jung's theory of personality types. They would observe people's speech patterns, mannerisms, and other behaviours in order to identify patterns that they believed corresponded to certain types.

At last, after intense editing and revisions, the MBTI® was officially commercially published in 1956 by Consulting Psychologists Press, Inc. This initial version of the MBTI® was first distributed to a few hundred people, including psychologists, educators, and business professionals.

Isabel first self-published a booklet called *Introduction to Type* in 1962 when the assessment was released. Later on, in 1980, she and her husband Peter co-published *Gifts Differing: Understanding Personality Type* to further explain the 16 personality types to

Swarthmore College, where the first version of the MBTI® was tested.

a global market. In 1985, the MBTI® Step II assessment was released, which provides more in-depth information about an individual's personality type. Their work has helped millions of people since then!

> 'The best-adjusted people are the "psychologically patriotic", who are glad to be what they are.'
> – Isabel Briggs Myers, *Gifts Differing: Understanding Personality Type*

The official MBTI® manuals have since undergone numerous revisions for clarity and consistency. Today, it is widely used by career coaches, counsellors, recruiters, human resources managers and organizational development professionals. Anyone who deals with people and jobs, basically.

The Keirsey Temperament Sorter

The Keirsey Temperament Sorter was created by American psychologist David Keirsey (1921–2013) in 1956. Keirsey developed an interest in personality psychology after World War II by reading American psychologist William Sheldon and German psychiatrist Ernst Kretschmer during the late 1940s. Keirsey said, 'Our attempts to reshape others may produce change, but the change is distortion rather than transformation.'

He reimagined Galen's four humours into his Temperament Sorter: *Artisan*, *Guardian*, *Idealist* and *Rational*. These temperaments loosely correlated with the Sensing – Perceiving (SP), Sensing – Judging (SJ), Intuitive – Feeling (NF) and Intuitive – Thinking (NT) personality types of Jung. To bring his vision to the world, Keirsey published *Please Understand Me* with Marilyn Bates in 1978.

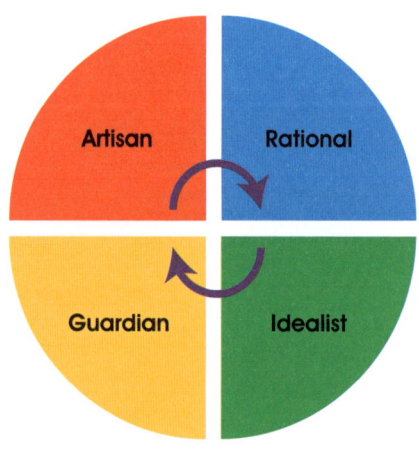

The Keirsey Temperament Sorter.

The Color Code Personality Profile

This similar but more simplified personality profile, also called *The Color Code* or *The People Code*, was later developed in the 1980s by American psychologist Taylor Hartman. His personality assessment contains 45 questions and is very similar to the DISC model of communication – i.e. Dominant (D) – Influencing (I) – Steady (S) – Consistent (C), which we talked about earlier.

It consists of four colours that symbolize different drives: Red (power), Blue (relationships), White (peace) and Yellow (fun). Both the Keirsey Temperament Sorter and the People Code have been commonly critiqued by psychologists as being overly simplistic in explaining the differences between people.

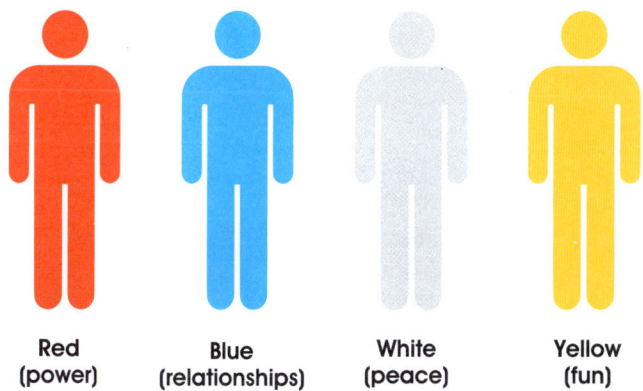

The Color Code Personality Profile.

Socionics

Socionics, a personality system that was conceived by Lithuanian researcher Aušra Augustinavičiūtė (1927–2005), sometimes shortened to Augusta, was devised in the 1970s. It involves 16 sociotypes, small groups and intertype relations. Augusta was dean of the Vilnius Pedagogical University's Department of Family Science, and an economist.

Socionics has since been debunked as a pseudoscience by the Russian Academy of Sciences, grouped among the likes of astrology. Interestingly, though, more than 150 Russian universities still teach Socionics as an alternative to the original Jungian theories. Its sheer complexity has made it difficult to grasp for a mainstream audience.

Aušra Augustinavičiūtė.

Jungian Type Index

To kick off the third millennium, Danish psychologists Thor Ødegård and Hallvard E. Ringstad proposed the Jungian Type Index (JTI) in 2001 after publishing *Typeforståelse: Jung's Typepsykologi* (tr: *Type Understanding: Jung's Type Psychology*) in 1999. This is still an active psychometric assessment company today, with a head office in Denmark. Its questions focus on the cognitive functions as opposed to the four Jungian preference scales (Introversion – Extraversion, Sensing – Intuition, Thinking – Feeling, Judging – Perceiving). It's most commonly administered in Scandinavian countries such as Norway and Sweden.

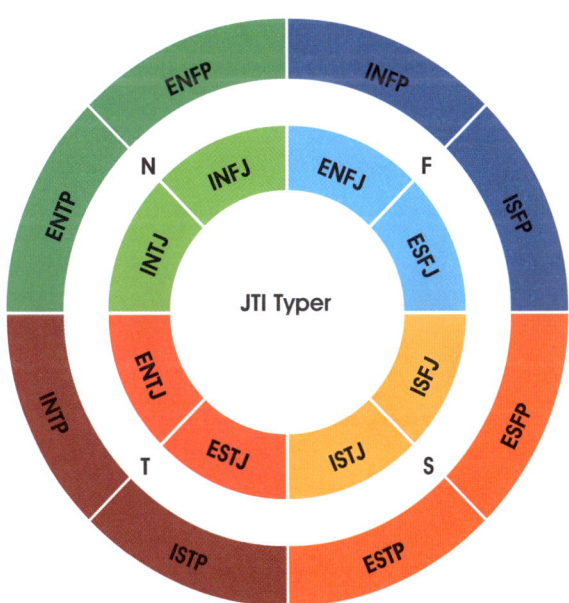

The Jungian Type Index.

Conclusion

As we can see, Carl Jung's work is still widely studied and discussed in personality theory courses at colleges and universities around the world. His influential personality theories are in constant motion, with applications in psychotherapy, occupational coaching, industrial and organizational (I/O) psychology and higher academia.

With further research and iterations, perhaps Jung's work will flourish into a comprehensive, universal personality assessment openly available to all. Even though he died in 1961, his brilliant mind and legacy live on. Thanks to Jung, we're left with a treasure trove of fascinating works and brilliant quotes.

The privilege of a lifetime is to become who you truly are.

Carl Jung's ideas about personality types remain incredibly influential today.

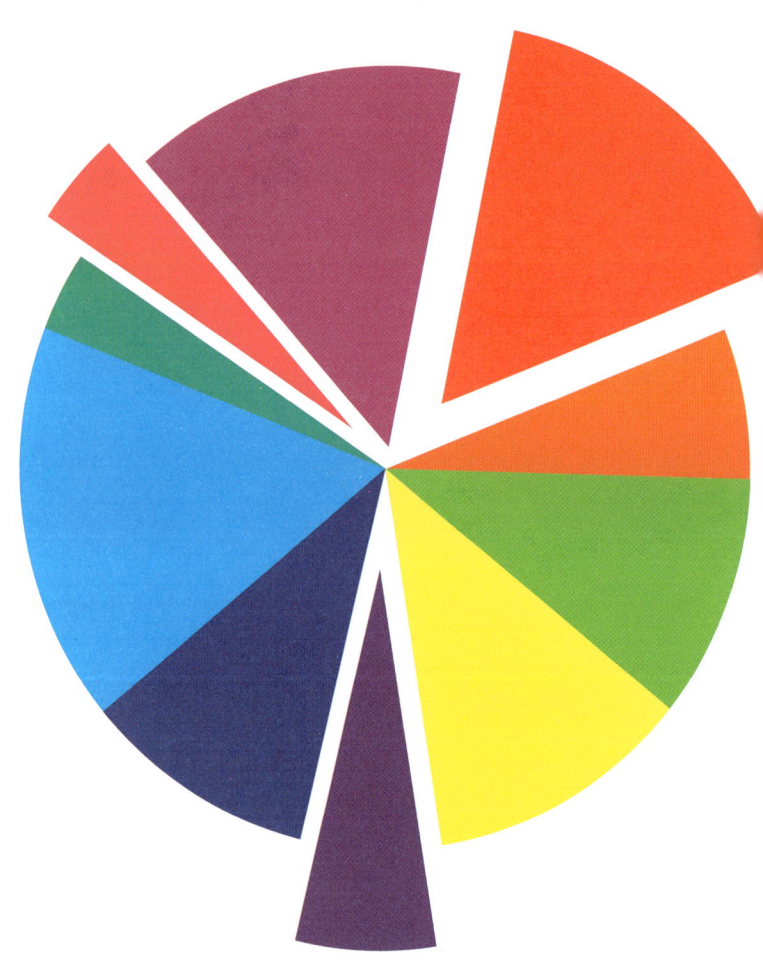

Personality Psychology Glossary

Archetype: The different psychic drivers that are assigned a particular role in human *motivation*.

Cognitive functions: Set of eight behaviour-based 'building blocks' that make up the differences between the 16 Jungian personality types.

Collective unconscious: A pool of psychic images and knowledge that is known to everyone, and is present at birth. It includes Jung's archetypes, which are present in dreams.

Ego: The second part to Freud's three-part model of the psyche, responsible for reality. It mediates the decisions of the id and superego.

Extraversion (E): The inclination to gain energy around other people and be preoccupied with the external world.

Extraverted Feeling (Fe): One of Jung's eight functions that deals with the external world. **Connecting** → Harmonizing with other people to feel a warm togetherness.

Extraverted Intuition (Ne): One of Jung's eight functions that deals with the external world. **Brainstorming** → Coming up with many possibilities of the future for numerous projects at once.

Extraverted Sensing (Se): One of Jung's eight functions that deals with the external world. **Experiencing** → Soaking in each moment using all five senses.

Extraverted Thinking (Te): One of Jung's eight functions that deals with the external world. **Evaluating** → Organizing a workday through schedules and tasks to maximize efficiency.

Feeling (F): The preference to make decisions based on how they'll affect other people, personal (subjective) values, and how one 'feels' towards the situation.

Four humours: Hippocrates and later Galen's theory of personality imbalance due to bodily fluids, namely *sanguine* (blood), *choleric* (yellow bile), *phlegmatic* (phlegm) and *melancholic* (black bile).

Id: The childlike and impulsive core of Freud's three-part model of the psyche, responsible for biological urges such as hunger and thirst.

Introversion (I): The inclination to gain energy alone and be preoccupied with the internal world of thoughts, ideas and feelings.

Introverted Feeling (Fi): One of Jung's eight functions that deals with the internal world. **Internalizing** → Understanding internal feelings to achieve value congruence and authenticity with actions.

Introverted Intuition (Ni): One of Jung's eight functions that deals with the internal world. **Envisioning** → Picturing the future and how it'll look from the inside out.

Introverted Sensing (Si): One of Jung's eight functions that deals with the internal world. **Recalling** → Remembering past details and comparing them to the present.

Introverted Thinking (Ti): One of Jung's eight functions that deals with the internal world. **Understanding** → Gathering data and theories to formulate a complete idea of a concept.

Intuition (N): The preference for hunches, 'a-ha!' moments and knowing through information and 'what could be' in terms of ideas.

Judging (J): The preference to meet (sometimes beat) deadlines, schedule events in advance and view time as a finite (and important) resource.

Likert scale: Linear set of responses with increasing or decreasing intensity, often ranging with options from Strongly Disagree to Strongly Agree.

Neurosis: Jung's term for abnormal psychological processing after trauma. It's now more commonly known as mental illness. He coined the term after being pushed to the ground and experiencing seizures.

Perceiving (P): The preference to keep options open 'in case' something better comes along, see deadlines as flexible and view time as an elastic resource.

Persona: The 'social mask' people wear in public to conceal certain parts of the true self, comparable to Freud's ego and superego.

Personality: Umbrella term for the traits, behaviours and preferences of an individual that stays *relatively consistent* over the course of time.

Personality trait: A characteristic or quality of an individual that distinguishes their character, for example: Agreeableness (A) from the Five Factor Model (FFM).

Personality type: A wrapped psychological box of personality traits that result in a select few types. Jung's theory resulted in 16 different personality types.

Psychology: Study of human behaviour and how we think, act and feel.

Psychometrics: The scientific design of personality tests to measure traits, as well as the interpretation of those collected results.

Sensing (S): The preference to take in information through the five senses: sight, touch, taste, hearing and smell; knowing through doing.

Sigmund Freud: Founding father of psychoanalysis and a prominent figure of interest to Carl Jung. The men met to discuss the field of psychotherapy before realizing there were conflicts in how they approached their research.

Superego: The third part to Freud's three-part model of the psyche, responsible for morality and doing what is 'right' in terms of ethics, and depending on the person and their religious values. It develops around age three to five in children.

Thinking (T): The preference to make decisions based on facts, statistics, pros and cons, and objectives.

Further Reading into Jung's Personality Types

Want to learn more about the Jungian personality types – its history and applications? Check out these reads to dive deeper into the mystical, deeply fascinating world of Jung, whose work has influenced many modern-day personality theories.

Of course, to start, we recommend the original *Psychological Types* by Jung himself, which was first published in 1921 and subsequently translated and republished many times. If this is too dense a read, see below for some fun options.

> Tieger, Paul D. and Barron-Tieger, Barbara, *Do What You Are: Discover the Perfect Career for You Through the Secrets of Personality Type* (Sphere, 2007)

Get hands-on and actionable advice from a career expert with a passion for personality type. The tone of this book is lighthearted and funny, making it a thoroughly enjoyable read. A self-test is included, which is perfect for anyone seeking to confirm their personality type or looking for a career change.

> Lachman, Gary, *Jung the Mystic: The Esoteric Dimensions of Carl Jung's Life and Teachings* (Penguin, 2010)

Remember how Jung used to have nightmares as a child? This book takes you through how the supernatural influenced his upbringing and work. It touches upon darker themes, which should thrill paranormal enthusiasts. Many psychological horror movie themes can be found here.

> Briggs Myers, Isabel, *Gifts Differing: Understanding Personality Type* (Davies Black Publishing, 1995)

The daughter of Katherine Cook Briggs wrote *the* book that would launch Jung's personality theories into the mainstream. This really packs a punch, and touches on compatibility, marriage, child development and learning styles.

> Daniels, Michael, *Self-Discovery the Jungian Way: The Watchword Technique* (Routledge, 2014)

Daniels brings self-analysis to a new level in this book, which explains Jung's concepts clearly to all psychology enthusiasts. It features numerous viewpoints on the Jungian archetypes in particular.

> Morbach, Ana and Da Silva Pedroso, Janari, 'The Stages of Life in the Jungian Perspective: A Photo Elicitation Case Study', *Journal of Clinical & Developmental Psychology* (2022). (doi: https://doi.org/10.13129/2612-4033/0110-3428)

This study goes through a series of thought-provoking photograph descriptions that capture the essence of the human condition, in relation to Jung's stages of life. It will help you learn more about ego complexes and what it means to progress through life.

Index

advertising 104
Agreeableness
　in personality trait theories 17
Allport, Gordon 12–13
archetypes 12, 30, 98–105, 119
Artisan temperament 112
Augustinavičiūtė, Aušra 114
Basel, University of 28
Bates, Marilyn 112
Briggs Myers, Isabel 108–11
Burghölzli Clinic 28, 29
Caregiver archetype 101, 1303
Cattell, Robin 12, 30
Character and Personality 12
Christal, Raymond 13
cognitive functions
　description of 119
　Extraverted Feeling (Fe) –
　　Connecting 68–9
　Extraverted Intuition (Ne) –
　　Brainstorming 59–61
　Extraverted Sensing (Se) –
　　Experiencing 55–7
　Extraverted Thinking (Te) –
　　Evaluating 63–5
　introvert and extrovert comparisons
　　51–2
　Introverted Feeling (Fi) –
　　Internalizing 65–7
　Introverted Intuition (Ni) –
　　Envisioning 57–9
　Introverted Sensing (Si) – Recalling
　　53–5
　Introverted Thinking (Ti) –
　　Understanding 61–3
　and Jungian family car metaphor
　　46–50
　in personality trait theories 22
collective unconscious 103, 119
Color Code Personality Profile 113
complexes 30
Conscientiousness
　in DISC assessment 13
　in personality trait theories 17
Cook Briggs, Katharine 108–11
Costa, P.T. 13
Creator archetype 101, 103
DISC assessment 13
Dominance
　in DISC assessment 13
ectomorphs 21
Ego
　as cardinal orientation 100, 102, 103
　description of 119
endomorphs 21
Explorer archetype 101, 103
Extraversion
　comparison with Introversion 51–2
　description of 119
　in personality trait theories 17
　trait in personality types 38
Extraverted Feelers (ESFJ & ENFJ)
　81–2, 83
Extraverted Feeling (Fe) – Connecting
　68–9, 80, 119
Extraverted Intuition (Ne) –
　Brainstorming 59–61, 84, 119–20
Extraverted Intuitives (ENFP &
　ENTP) 84–6
Extraverted Sensing (Se) –
　Experiencing 55–7, 83, 120
Extraverted Sensors (ESFP & ESTP)
　82, 83–4
Extraverted Thinkers (ESTJ & ENTJ)
　78–80
Extraverted Thinking (Te) – Evaluating
　63–5, 78, 120
Feeling
　description of 120
　trait in personality types 39–40
Five-Factor Model (FFM) 13, 17–18
four cardinal orientations 100
four humours 19–21, 75, 112, 120
four scales of 16 personality types
　36–43
Freedom

as cardinal orientation 100, 101, 103
Freud, Sigmund 30, 31, 122
Fromm, Erich 33
Galen of Pergamon 20, 75, 112
Galton, Sir Francis 12
General Medical Society for Psychotherapy 33
Gifts Differing: Understanding Personality Type (Myers and Briggs Myers) 110, 111
Guardian temperament 112
Hartman, Taylor 113
Hero archetype 102, 103
Hippocrates 19–20
Id 120
Idealist temperament 112
Influence
    in DISC assessment 13
Innocent archetype 101, 103
'Instinct and the Unconscious' (Jung) 12
Introduction to Type (Briggs Myers) 110
Introversion
    comparison with Extraversion 51–2
    description of 120
    trait in personality types 37
Introverted Feelers (ISFP & INFP) 89–91
Introverted Feeling (Fi) – Internalizing 65–7, 89, 120
Introverted Intuition (Ni) – Envisioning 57–9, 120
Introverted Intuitives (INFJ & INTJ) 95
Introverted Sensing (Si) – Recalling 53–5, 91, 121
Introverted Sensors (ISFJ & ISTJ) 91–3
Introverted Thinkers (ISTP & INTP) 87–9
Introverted Thinking (Ti) – Understanding 61–3, 87, 121
Intuition
    description of 121
    trait in personality types 38
James, William 75

Jester archetype 102, 103
Judging
    description of 121
    trait in personality types 40
Jung, Carl
    best-fit personality type theory 18, 72–3
    influence of 108–16
    life and work of 26–33, 119
    and personality psychology 12
    personality trait theories 22
    on personality types 72–6
Jung, Paul 27
Jungian Type Index (JTI) 115
Kant, Immanuel 76
Keirsey, David 112
Keirsey Temperament Sorter 112, 113
Kretschmer, Ernst 112
Likert scale 16, 121
Lover archetype 102, 103
Magician archetype 102, 103, 104
Maslow, Abraham 72
McCrae, R.R. 13
Meet Yourself Using the Personality Paint Box (Cook Briggs) 109
Member archetype 102, 103
mesomorphs 21
Minnesota Multiphasic Personality Inventory (MMPI) 30
Myers–Briggs Type Indicator 36, 108–11
Myers, Peter 110
Neuroticism
    description of 121
    in personality trait theories 18
Odbert, Henry 12–13
Ødegård, Thor 115
'On the Psychology and Pathology of So-Called Occult Phenomena' (Jung) 30
Openness
    in personality trait theories 17
Order
    as cardinal orientation 100, 101, 103
Ostwald, Wilhelm 75

Outlaw archetype 102, 103
Perceiving
  description of 121
  trait in personality types 41
persona 121
personality
  descriptions of 10, 121
  history of personality psychology 12–13
personality traits 17, 18, 22, 122
personality types 36–43, 72–6, 122
Please Understand Me (Bates and Keirsey) 112
Psychological Types (Jung) 12, 26, 30, 36, 72–5, 108, 119
Psychology of Dementia Praecox, The (Jung) 30
Psychology of the Unconscious (Jung) 30
Rational temperament 112
Ringstad, Hallvard E. 115
Ruler archetype 101, 103
Sage archetype 101, 103
Sheldon, William Herbert 21
Sensing
  description of 122
  trait in personality types 38
Sheldon, William 112
16 Personality Factors model 13, 30
16 personality types
  four factors of 36–43
  Jung on 72–6
Social
  as cardinal orientation 100, 102, 103
Socionics 114
Steadiness
  in DISC assessment 13
stereotypes 42–3
stress, reactions to 10
Studies in Word Association (Jung) 30
superego 122
synchronicities 30
Thinking
  description of 122
  trait in personality types 38–9
three body theory 21–2
Tupes, Ernest 13
Type Understanding: Jung's Type Psychology (Ødegård and Ringstad) 115

Picture credits

t = top, b = bottom

Adobe Stock: 123

Alamy: 20, 114

Shutterstock: 8, 9, 10, 11, 13, 18, 19 (x2), 21, 32, 33, 36, 37, 39, 40, 41, 43 (x2), 46, 48, 49, 52 (x2), 54, 55, 56, 57, 58, 59, 60 (x2), 62, 63, 64, 65, 66, 67, 68, 69, 72, 73, 74, 77, 79, 81, 82, 85, 88, 90, 93, 94, 98, 99, 105, 110

Wikimedia Commons: 12, 16, 26, 27, 28, 29, 31, 76, 109, 117